Sponges
Spectacular Sea Creatures

by
Laura Sue Perricone

Sponges
Spectacular Sea Creatures
Original Watercolor Illustrations by Laura Sue Perricone
Copyright 2018 by Laura S. Perricone
A Lullaby & Learn™ Book
ISBN - 13: 978-1725807600
ISBN - 10: 1725807602
All rights reserved. No part of this publication may be reproduced, distributed, or transmitted in any form or by any means including photocopying, recording, or other electronic or mechanical methods without permission in writing from

Welcome to Lullaby & Learn™ Books for Children

Lullaby & Learn™ Books provide a dynamic and multi-layered learning experience for children as they grow and develop.

Children are naturally curious. Providing as many 'hands-on' experiences as possible for exploration through the 5 senses is crucial. Why? It paves the way for conceptualization and the ability to mentally visualize what is read. In addition to hands-on exploration, guided learning is required. Guided learning draws on early learning experiences that hands-on opportunities provide. As children develop, the interplay of the sensorial and the conceptual facilitate further learning.

You may be familiar with the first Lullaby & Learn™ Book in the series called, *"What Color, Quilly?"*. The lyrical narrative, colorful illustrations, along with the interactive element serve to lay the foundation for language development and pre-reading skills. The illustrations present a rich context that helps young ones make the connection among the sounds of words, the letters that represent the sounds that form the words and a context from which to glean meaning, all of which are prerequisites for success in Reading later on.

With repeated readings, children grasp more of the 'hidden' learning features and become proficient in completing the tasks that layered learning offers. The uniqueness of Lullaby & Learn Books is that they bridge the gap from what has already been learned to the acquisition of new skills. As new skills are mastered, self-confidence grows. All this is accomplished seamlessly over time. Timing and patience are very important because children learn best in their own way at a pace that's right for them. That is why, unlike other children's books, Lullaby & Learn™ Books are designed to be read, not one time as you would a storybook, although L & L books have endearing characteristics of a storybook, but rather as a 'listen-learn-do' book. So, if your toddler, or six-year old says, "we already read that", simply say it's a "Re-visit Book". Soon you will see their progress. What is more exciting than that!

How to know your child is making progress? That's a good question. Be observant. Your child will exhibit behaviors that indicate progress is being made. Let's use "What Color, Quilly?" for example. Your child may finish the verse before you do, having learned the verses from memory; or blurt-out the name of the color before you finish asking the question. They may identify words by sight and point to them. They may take over the role of 'teacher' and quiz you! Other behaviors include making-up a story to go along with the illustration or raising questions that indicate they want to learn more about animals, for instance, or airplanes. Be on the lookout for signs of progress and acknowledge it with specific and sincere praise and, of course, a smile or hug. This feeling of accomplishment is what builds self-confidence and spurs them on. And as we know, self-confidence is the cornerstone for success in Reading and in life.

Sponges: Spectacular Sea Creatures is another Lullaby & Learn™ Book with multi-layered learning built-in. It presents factual information about nature under the sea in a format designed to increase Reading Comprehension. Reading comprehension is an important skill at any age. Wouldn't you agree?

To build and increase this skill, we need to go back to basics, something everyone is familiar with – The 5 W's plus, How? They are, "Who, What, When, Where, Why and How." These questions get to the heart of the topic. The ability to recognize these important questions when they're not so obvious is absolutely necessary to fully understand and retain what we read. Simple? Yes, and very effective.

If your child is able to read independently, some preliminary instructions are necessary. Model the skill for them. Open up to the first page of the narrative and call their attention to the fact that some questions will be as obvious as the 1st question. Then tell them that there are some hidden questions that are more difficult to identify. Explain how to use the 5 W's plus How to help them remember what they read. Teach them a little tip that may make it easier to detect an indirect (hidden) question: "After reading a sentence, ask yourself, 'What question is it answering?' Do one together verbalizing your thinking process and then have them find a hidden question embedded in the text.

If you are reading the book with a young child, introduce the method by telling them that asking questions is good –That's how we learn. As in the example above, model the process and then tell them that you'll play a little game of 'finding the question' as you read to them. When you come to a hidden question, stop, and say, "I wonder what question that information is asking?" For a near-reader, you may even make flashcards with each 'W' or 'How' and let them choose. Or, turn the answer around for them, and ask, "What question is 'such and such' answering?" Keep it simple and matter of fact. For much younger children, simply tell them the question it answers. They will get the idea as you model. Revisit the skill again at another time. The more you "Revisit", the more opportunities there are for learning.

Most importantly, make it fun! Stop at the appropriate time and do a fun activity to end the session. Have ready some sponges and paint and do some Sponge Art. (Ideas are toward the back of the book).

Check-in with your independent reader from time to time to see their progress and celebrate it! Then, perhaps, together plan a Sponge-Art Party with friends!

"Learning becomes a very pleasant journey when you have the right tools to work with."
~Laura

For Isabelle

SPONGES
Spectacular Creatures of the Sea

What are sea sponges?

Sea sponges are animals.

That's right! But they have no head, eyes, mouth, ears, or heartbeat – No tails either. They have no brain or nervous system.

Sponges have pores, or holes, that allow water to flow freely through them all the time. That is why the general name for sponges is Phylum Porifera (Fi-luhm Poor-i-fair-uh). It means 'pore-bearing'.

Most sponges live underwater in the oceans. Although, some species live in fresh water.

Sponges don't swim around like fish or turtles. Rather, they attach themselves to rocks, coral reefs, or shell beds and that is where they remain.

There are more than 9,000 species worldwide and they come in all colors, shapes, and sizes. Some are as tiny as your pinky finger. The largest are between 3 feet and 6 feet!

The stove-pipe sponge, for example, can grow up to 5 feet tall and 3 inches thick. Can you identify the stove-pipe sponge?

Phylum Porifera

What do sponges eat?

Not people food! And not 3 meals a day!

Sponges eat small particles floating in the water called plankton (plank-ton) In addition to these microscopic organisms, they also eat bacteria, and other organic, or living, organisms. Water flows continuously through the sponge's pores carrying the food particles. The food is filtered out providing the sponge with an endless supply of food to eat 24 hours a day.

This also helps the environment. We'll find out how, later.

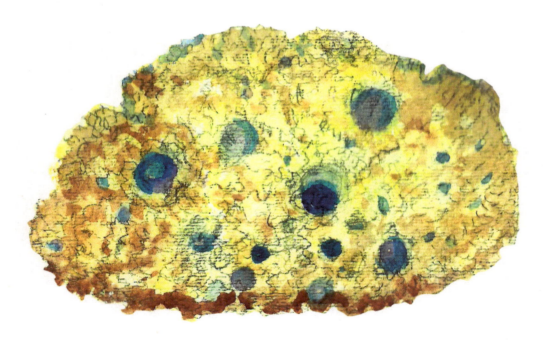

Water flows freely through the pores

Why are some sponges tall?
How do they remain upright in strong currents?

Sponges have a skeleton that gives them shape and protects them from predators. But their skeleton is not like ours – Oh-no. They don't have bones like we do. Their skeleton is formed from other materials called spicules (spik-yoo-uhls). Spicules are so tiny, you need a microscope to see them. Some spicules are made of minerals and silica, the same material found in glass and it is very strong, strong enough to stand tall and not be torn away by strong currents.

Other spicules are made of a substance called, "spongin". Spongin is a protein that forms a network of tiny fibers that crisscross and mesh together. This pattern not only makes them strong, but flexible and soft as well. Have you noticed what happens when you squeeze a wet sponge and then release it? It returns to its natural shape. Why? Because its spicules are made of spongin.

Scientists identify sponges by looking at their spicules under a microscope.

Engineers study the structure of spicules because they are so strong. Why? To get ideas for improving building designs and using materials that are better able to withstand high winds and flood waters that cause tremendous damage.

Meet the Venus' Flower Basket Sponge.

The Venus' Flower Basket Sponge contains spicules made from silica. These glass spicules are able to trap and transport light deep inside the sponge by way of its fiber-optic like spicules. Think of it as a nightlight in a darkened room.

Now, look closely at the illustration. Can you guess what is inside?

Surprise! The Venus' Flower Basket Sponge is home to a pair of tiny shrimps! It's a happy arrangement. The sponge provides food and shelter for the shrimps, and the shrimps keep the interior of the sponge clean. This is called, a symbiotic (sim-bee-ah-tic) relationship. Each benefit from what the other provides.

When the shrimps have offspring, the young shrimps will leave their parents' home to go find a Venus' Flower Basket Sponge of their very own.

Venus' Flower Basket Sponge

Where do sponges live?

Sponges live in bodies of water all around the globe from the far polar regions to the equator.

Most of the sponges that we are familiar with come from the tropic regions where the water temperature is warm, places like the Mediterranean.

For example, Tarpon Springs, on the Gulf coast of Florida, is a city famous for its sea sponges.

Around the early 1900's Greek immigrants came and settled in Tarpon Springs. They used their skills of sponge diving to build a thriving industry there. Today, people from all over the world visit the quaint sponge dock area of Tarpon Springs in the warm waters of the Gulf of Mexico. There they learn about the history of sponge diving and take boat tours to see the sights. They sample Greek food in the locally owned restaurants, and shop in the stores and boutiques along the cobblestone streets where Greek is still spoken.

Sponge Docks in Tarpon Springs, Florida

How are sponges harvested (gathered)?

Experienced Divers harvest sponges. The Sea Captain knows the waters very well and takes the divers out to where the sponges are located. Remember, sponges are attached to underwater rocks, coral reefs, and shell beds, so it takes skill for divers to accomplish their work safely.

Divers wear special gear to go into the depths of the water. They have an air hose and a rope that keeps them tethered to the boat. The sponge diver's suit is made of waterproofed canvas material. The traditional helmet is made of copper or bronze, and the boots are weighted to help the divers stay submerged while they gather the sponges. Altogether, an outfit can weigh close to 200 pounds!

When divers reach the sponges, they cut each one carefully leaving some of it attached so it will re-grow for another harvest. Sometimes a small piece of sponge breaks off and drifts with the current until it attaches to something stationary. Then, it begins growing and forms another sponge. This is called "budding".

As divers gather sponges, they place them in nets. Once the nets are full, they bring them to the surface where they are hauled into the boat. The Sea Captain then returns to the docks and soon the sponges are taken to a factory where they go through a process. The hard outer-shell is removed, and they are cleaned and sorted. Some are cut-down to smaller sizes. After this, they are ready to be distributed to shops and stores to be sold to you and me.

Divers harvest sea sponges

Why are sponges important for the environment?

Sponges are a renewable resource from the sea.

All species of sponges are an important part of the Ecosystem (ee-koh-sis-tem). Think of the Ecosystem as a large city where plant and marine life live in harmony together. Every inhabitant, whether plant or animal, is an important part of the Ecosystem, each contributing something beneficial for the over-all well-being of every member of the 'city'.

A few pages back, it mentioned that sponges help the environment. Now, we'll find out exactly how. Can you guess? I'll give you a hint. They do something we do at home when we separate items in the trash. It begins with the letter 'R'.

If you said, 'Recycle', you are correct. Sponges are known as the 'recyclers' of the coral reefs in the underwater 'city'. They recycle organic matter to feed snails, crabs and thousands of marine plants and animals that depend on coral reefs for survival. Think of all the colorful corals, the varieties of fish, all the lobsters, clams, seahorses, and sea turtles! And these are only some of the varied life forms that live in and around the 'city'. The marine ecosystem is very important to the environment.

As underwater plants and animals work together to keep the delicate balance of our oceans healthy, they could still use our help. Can you think of ways in which people can help?

Coral Reef in the Gulf of Mexico

How are sponges used?

Sponges have many, many uses.

Did you know that scientists discovered that sponges contain compounds that can help people and animals? That's right! New medicines for diseases, and possibly cures, may be found with continued scientific research of our animal friends, the sea sponges.

Sponges are naturally good for cleaning as you may already know. Sponges are able to absorb lots of water and they are strong and durable. Although there are many types of sponges, the most popular are the 'wool' or 'silk' sponges, 'yellow' sponges, and 'grass' sponges. The spongin spicules in these make them ideal for cleaning and bathing. Sponges make bath-time such fun. Just a little bit of soap makes lots and lots of lather, and sponges are soft enough for babies' delicate skin. That is why new products are being made from these amazing animals.

Sponges are great for washing all kinds of things: cars, boats, floors, dishes, outdoor furniture, backyard slides and toys to name only some. And don't forget – They are good for washing your dog, too!

More uses for Sea Sponges

Sponges are also used in creating Art.

Artists use sponges to produce a variety of effects on many different surfaces; canvas, glass, ceramics, fabric, and buildings. Yes!

Painting with sponges is so much fun! If you can pick up a sponge, you can paint!

Sponge painting is a trendy way to personalize all kinds of things; furniture, to customize a picture frame, or clothing like T-shirts, sneakers, tote bags, backpacks, caps, lunch boxes, cards and making your own wrapping paper. The ideas are endless!

Sponges are also used to decorate because they are beautiful all by themselves. So why not use them to decorate your room. Create a nautical theme indoors or out. Use a fisherman's net as a backdrop or place a sponge on a book shelf or desk.

Ready for some fun activities? Turn the page.

~SPONGE ART SEARCH CHALLENGE

Look for all the artwork created with sponges from cover to cover. Look closely, you might be surprised! Invite a friend to play along. Who will find the most?

~Throw a SPONGE ART PARTY!

Invite friends for an afternoon of fun, indoors or out. Create something awesome together! Get ready, set, let's paint! Here's what you'll need.

Sponges of any size or shape, paint (water colors or acrylics), paper (white or tinted), some paper plates, paper towels and a bowl of water, some plastic spoons for stirring.

To get started, spread your materials out on a flat surface. Wet your sponges and squeeze the water out until they are damp. Now you're ready to begin.

~Create fluffy floating clouds

To make fluffy floating clouds, start with a sheet of tinted paper, or paint your own background sky and let it dry. Place a small amount of white acrylic paint on a paper plate and add only a drop or two of water and stir. Press your damp sponge into the paint and then dab it on your sky where ever you'd like a cloud. Then, rinse the sponge, squeeze it damp, and drag it lightly across the bottom of each cloud. See the sky come to life!

~Create underwater currents.

Mix a little blue, green, or turquoise acrylic or watercolor paint with a few drops of water. Turn the sheet of paper upside down and begin at the top. You'll see why later. Dip the flat side of a damp sponge into the paint. Drag it across in wavy strokes from one side to the other. Then, add a drop more water and paint another wave by overlapping the previous one, slightly. Continue adding a few more drops of water making a thinner paint for each wave. When you've run out of space, turn the paper right side up and let it dry. Notice the darker color waves toward the bottom add depth to the ocean. Now you can go on to create an underwater scene. Dab-in colorful sea sponges at the bottom of 'your ocean' or make a coral reef.

~Add a sea turtle.

Look at your sponges to find a half-circle shape or ask an adult to trim the sponge to a half-circle. Place a dab of brown and green paint onto a paper plate with a tiny bit of water because you need a thicker paint for the turtle's shell. Mix colors only slightly to create a mottled effect. Hold the sponge with the straight edge toward the bottom and press into the paint. Make sure the entire sponge is covered. Decide where your turtle should go and press down firmly with the palm of your hand. Carefully lift the sponge. Add head, arms, legs, tail, and there you have it - A sea turtle!

~Create delicate flowers, Autumn leaves, or colorful designs.

Use the tip, sides, and edges of the sponge to make blossoms, leaves, bushes or berries. Try assorted shapes to get other effects. Use all the colors on your palette. The possibilities are endless.

Now that you know the "Who, What, When, Where, Why and How" about sea sponges, wouldn't you agree---
> Sponges are truly SPECTACULAR!

The End